STOP
Being
Mr.Perfect

10 Practical Tips to Achieve Imperfection.

LAKSHMI SAGAR G

DEDICATION

The book “**STOP Being Mr. Perfect**” is dedicated to all the readers. I personally thank my parents, my teachers, my brother, my close ones, and my friends.

Copyright

About Author

Lakshmi Sagar G is currently pursuing a Ph.D. in Physics. He draws inspiration from renowned self-help authors. His passion for reading these influential thinkers fueled his interest in writing, which he began developing during his college years.

In 2017, driven by a desire to inspire and uplift others, he launched his motivational website aimed at helping individuals achieve their goals. Over the years, he has cultivated extensive blogging experience, particularly crafting short motivational articles. His writing focuses on work motivation, goal setting, productivity, overcoming procrastination, resilience in the face of failure, and pursuing dreams. His articles have gained widespread popularity on platforms like Reddit, where readers appreciate his relatable and encouraging insights. Lakshmi Sagar G's primary aim is to motivate and guide people toward building fulfilling and successful lives.

As a self-published author, he has released several works on platforms such as Amazon, Google Play, Notion Press, and Draft2Digital. His ebooks have reached an impressive milestone, with over one lakh copies downloads across platforms like Google Play Books and Amazon. His work has received thousands of positive reviews from readers, attesting to the impact his writing has had on their lives.

Below, you will find glowing reviews that reflect readers' value in his motivational guidance.

Reviews from readers of the author's previous books

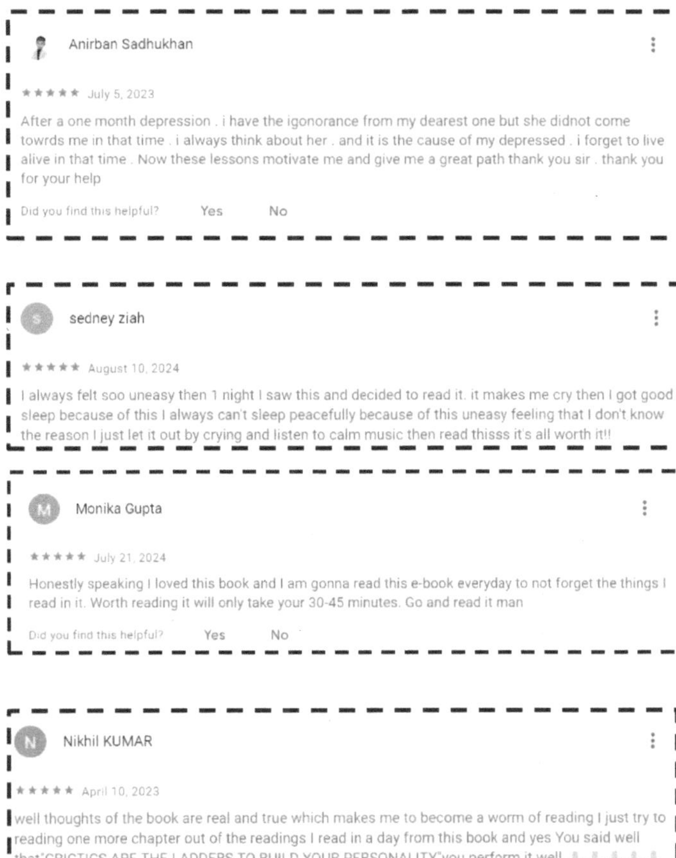

Anirban Sadhukhan

★★★★★ July 5, 2023

After a one month depression . i have the igonorance from my dearest one but she didnot come towrds me in that time . i always think about her . and it is the cause of my depressed . i forget to live alive in that time . Now these lessons motivate me and give me a great path thank you sir . thank you for your help

Did you find this helpful? Yes No

sedney ziah

★★★★★ August 10, 2024

I always felt soo uneasy then 1 night I saw this and decided to read it. it makes me cry then I got good sleep because of this I always can't sleep peacefully because of this uneasy feeling that I don't know the reason I just let it out by crying and listen to calm music then read thisss it's all worth it!!

Monika Gupta

★★★★★ July 21, 2024

Honestly speaking I loved this book and I am gonna read this e-book everyday to not forget the things I read in it. Worth reading it will only take your 30-45 minutes. Go and read it man

Did you find this helpful? Yes No

Nikhil KUMAR

★★★★★ April 10, 2023

well thoughts of the book are real and true which makes me to become a worm of reading I just try to reading one more chapter out of the readings I read in a day from this book and yes You said well that"CRICTICS ARE THE LADDERS TO BUILD YOUR PERSONALITY"you perform it well 🙏🙏🙏🙏🙏🙏🙏🙏🙏🙏🙏🙏🙏🙏 THANYOU SO LAKSMISAGAR JI FOR THIS BOOK AND I HOPE I YOU PROVIDE MORE BOOKS FOR LEADING US FROM DARKNEES TO LIGHT . THANK YOU SO MUCH.

Simran Fatima

★★★★★ October 22, 2023

What an impeccable book is this , certainly I m relating this book so much because I was running from my fear since very long , but when I read that paragraph that , you will have to face your fear one day , i just got a energy from that , so thank you very much I loved it

Did you find this helpful? Yes No

andukuri hasini

★★★★★ March 12, 2024

it's really a great book for teenager who are slowly losing their confidence about their great thoughts. I had read only half book, but as a teenager I can tell that it's building my confident Try this book...

Abuzar Ajaz

★★★★★ June 3, 2023

I really love it, I never read the before but this book give me so much energy now I have a good positive energy i really appreciate the author who made this book for free,bcz I couldn't afford such expenses, thanku so muchhh

Rajiv Raymarno Oliphant

★★★ June 23, 2023

Whilst obvious to notice that English is not the writers first language, The book provides alot of valuable information and touches on the key aspects of Self Development, Hard Work and daily life. At the same time also giving a realistic view on how one should approach life and enjoy it. Good Read.

Olebogeng Mokwena

★★★★ February 17, 2024

I just finished reading the book and it's a great book. I look forward to applying the lessons in my reality. The English used in the book book can be improved but I liked it

Did you find this helpful? Yes No

Ada walking Emils

★★★★ August 31, 2023

This book has taught me at least over 6 lessons that I myself have never even heard of before. The lessons in this book has improved my life to the extent that I feel more calm and the changes within my lifestyle. Overall, I recommend this book if you need a dozen or 2 lessons for life.

Did you find this helpful? Yes No

Anshu Kashyap

★★★★ July 23, 2023

every lines are most power full. Its full of positive lines. fully motivational book. mind-blowing line

Did you find this helpful? Yes No

lene chio

★★★★★ October 28, 2023

I really love how genuine the writer to his readers. All the best!

Did you find this helpful? Yes No

Sudesh

★★★★★ June 29, 2023

I have no words about this amazing book. I am so glad to get this chance to develop myself. The quotes of this book is really mind boggling and change my thoughts about life. I thankful to the narrator of this book. I think this is very good opportunity for youngster's coz this life changing book is free of cost. I am very grateful to get a chance to change my thoughts about life with the help of this book so, this is the reason, I gave five out of five to this book. Hats'of

Did you find this helpful? Yes No

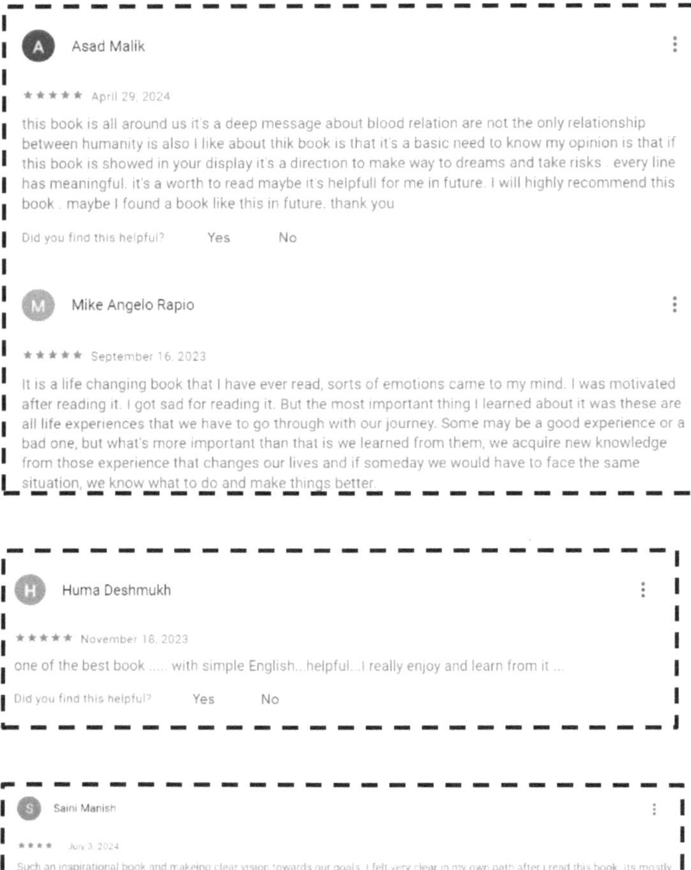

A Asad Malik

★★★★★ April 29, 2024

this book is all around us it's a deep message about blood relation are not the only relationship between humanity is also I like about thik book is that it's a basic need to know my opinion is that if this book is showed in your display it's a direction to make way to dreams and take risks . every line has meaningful. it's a worth to read maybe it's helpfull for me in future. I will highly recommend this book . maybe I found a book like this in future. thank you

Did you find this helpful? Yes No

M Mike Angelo Rapio

★★★★★ September 16, 2023

It is a life changing book that I have ever read, sorts of emotions came to my mind. I was motivated after reading it. I got sad for reading it. But the most important thing I learned about it was these are all life experiences that we have to go through with our journey. Some may be a good experience or a bad one, but what's more important than that is we learned from them, we acquire new knowledge from those experience that changes our lives and if someday we would have to face the same situation, we know what to do and make things better.

H Huma Deshmukh

★★★★★ November 18, 2023

one of the best book ..... with simple English...helpful...I really enjoy and learn from it ...

Did you find this helpful? Yes No

S Saini Manish

★★★★ July 3, 2024

Such an inspirational book and makeing clear vision towards our goals. I felt very clear in my own path after i read this book. its mostly helps people who suffers from self doubt , work stress , and being engaged through there own thoughts.

Did you find this helpful? Yes No

Preface

Note:- 1. Be aware reading this may make you imperfect.

2. It is a quick read and straight to the point, not wasting much time.

Everybody likes Mr.Perfect, and everybody's dream is to become Mr.Perfect. Like everyone, I also like Mr. Perfects. I personally don't have any enmity about perfectionism.

But how many people can we see as perfectionist?

Rarely a few blessed souls who worked hard to achieve it. But the rest are ordinary people who want to become Mr.Perfect. In the process, they will surrender to procrastination, overthinking, fear, stress, anxiety, and unproductive things. We must identify that thin difference. This book aims to help those stuck in this situation and guide them to a better life.

“Welcome. All the Best, and I hope you may like this book.”

CONTENTS

"The most valuable thing you can make is a mistake. You can't learn anything from being perfect."

- Adam Osborne

No One is Perfect

No one is perfect in this world. Everyone has their flaws. All the human beings make mistakes. These mistakes only open us to a light of knowledge, which in return becomes success. Ask the world's number one batsman, "Are you a perfect batsman?". He will indeed say he is not, and there are more things he wants to learn till now. Even the world's greatest batsman became "ducks out" sometimes. As time varies, strike rate varies from match to match and pitch to pitch. It means our nature is not ready to give us perfectionism. We can go near perfectionism through effort and practice, but we can't achieve it altogether.

Why mistakes will happen?

Mistakes will definitely happen when we want to learn new things. For example, if I put you in a known place and tell you to reach someplace in 10 minutes, you can achieve it effortlessly. But when I put you in an unknown place and ask you to go someplace in the same 10 minutes, chances are you can take more time to reach. It's the exact distance and same time, but why not the same results? It is because of the known and unknown. To know the unknown, it is expected to make mistakes. These mistakes will only direct us to the destination place.

You may ask me, other than my work, why I learn so many new things. It is a good question, but I am discussing new things related to your work. It may be a subpart of your work, so try to explore that part and expand your learning by doing this. Here, mistakes will happen again, but try to accept them. Some people will think it a shame to make mistakes and don't accept them. The day you receive them, it opens you to new learning that gives you knowledge. That knowledge can help you master your field.

"We can not make mistakes; it will happen. Don't be embarrassed about what you have not done."

Identify the Nature's Gift

Since there is no particular way to do something, I say no perfection exists. Even though there is no specific way to acquire knowledge, it may also come in different forms. As a receiver end, we have to identify it in its way, and we should receive it with a warm welcome. Nature has given us a tremendous magical miracle called "mind" to us. The only point is, how much do we use it for our benefit?

The world is like a classroom, and nature is like a good teacher. It teaches the same for all, but only intelligent students can grasp it to make them better. There is a difference between seeing and observing; there is a difference between hearing and listening. Our brain is involved in seeing and hearing, but in observing and listening, our mind gets involved. That is a significant difference. Our mind has infinite energy; an average human can only use it for limited things. For the best example, a physically challenged person uses other sense organs to learn. They can learn many different things from this as well. It doesn't mean we can't learn anything if one thing fails. Just like one door closes, many other doors will open. There is no end to it.

We can learn by observing, we can learn by listening, we can learn by doing, and we can learn by mistakes. My point is that I don't think I am doing everything perfectly. If you do, then well and good, but don't worry if you fail. Every possible thing we can't imagine before, and some things are behind our imagination. However, some work needs practical realization as well. It is like a science experiment; you can predict the result if you know some parameters. But tomorrow, we don't know which error will induce it and may not get the desired results. That means we should not think we are imperfect; instead, we must focus our energy on our problems to find solutions. Don't be worried about perfection here. Instead, do the things first and fail to learn new things. That is the way of success.

"The speed of any achievement will be directly proportional to how quickly you make mistakes and fail, and you will learn from them."

Detaching Our Mind from Unuseful Things

In the process of doing everything correctly, our brain consumes more time. Giving as much time as needed to finish that task is necessary. But sometimes, perfectionism turns out to be stressful procrastination. To explain, if I give you a task to complete in one month, you divide that one month into 30 days and assign yourself a tiny task every day. You take more time to search and collect the data, and so does that task. However, I know that the task needs only 3 days to complete. Although I have given you an extra

27 days for quality work. My question is, can I get better quality work by giving you additional time?

A biker can easily cover 50 Km for one hour on a highway road. If I give him 1 day then, what he can do? It applies to every task you do. Giving more time to our tasks means our brain automatically thinks more about that work. It is good in some cases and not applicable to all the cases. I am talking about a different case. Perfectionism sometimes becomes an unbearable addiction. It makes people over-thinkers. A state where you will not be satisfied with your work. When you compare your work to yours, it becomes stressful for no reason. Every time you postpone your work because you are unsatisfied with that. The problem with this is that you can complete 10 tasks a month, but you will be stuck on only one task, expecting it to be world-class work. Every work does not deserve your valuable time. It consumes the powerful focusing energy of our mind in an unuseful thing. By this, our thoughts day and night work for that task. It creates stress, and it affects the other parts of our lifestyles as well. It leads to an unhappy life. I am not telling you not to give 100% of yourself, but give it in bounded time. Give time to every task as it needs, not more or less.

“ If you think too much about a problem, it doesn’t mean you will solve it by just thinking. Take some actions.”

Attaining the State of Automaticity

We have to give less time, but how much? Who decides that?

For this, I propose that you practice "**Open-eye meditation**." You may be thinking about what this open-eye meditation is.

You may be imagining doing meditation with open eyes. Is this not the way we can do this? I mean, "open-eye meditation" is the consciousness we give while doing any work. Give the time it deserves for the work and provide the focus it demands. An intense focus can teach you multiple things at a time, and our minds have the potential to learn this.

Practice this intense laser-like focus. By focusing, you can reduce the time you need to complete the task. For example, if any task takes a day on the first attempt to finish, then try this same task to finish it with minimum time. Give thoughts to your mind every day with the consciousness of completing that task early and preserving the quality of work. Believe me, a miracle happens when your focused thoughts work for a single goal.

But practicing this mindset is not easy. It is just like a meditation in a practical world. Many distractions may trouble you, and you may also lose focus. But when you fail, come back and start the task from the beginning.

Don't stop until you achieve this state. If you train your mind every day or every minute like this, then there may be a possibility of achieving this mindset. Overthinking is negative, and it diverts our energy to less productive areas. The key point is to avoid negative things daily and walk towards positivity.

Following this lets you see how effortlessly and effectively you do that task. More time is needed initially, but doing it in less time becomes automatic. It is the significantly less time you are giving with more satisfaction. Trust me, a calm mind can solve any problem.

"A conscious, calm mind knows the fulfillment."

An Opportunist Way of Thinking

If you think 100 times correctly about some situations, the 101st time may not be in your hand because thoughts are imaginary and just predictions. It may or may not happen accordingly. However, the one action regarding that work may give you many things about it. Don't bury the problems without doing the practical stuff.

One of my teachers used to say, "Don't be afraid of the complexity of the problem. If that problem comes to you, then you have all the possibilities to solve it. That's the only reason that problem came to you. It came to you to realize your inner problem." Yes, it was true readers. Only difficult times can make us better and extract precious things from us. It came to us to create the strongest warrior. Don't turn your back on your problems or suppress your potential in useless thought. Give a call to your mind to take action. Be practical because sometimes our thoughts may fail to predict the results of actions. Yes, it is essential to put in constant effort. It is important to practice this. Because this action will definitely give you the satisfaction of doing that work, it is much less time needed to complete a task than thinking about it. You will be satisfied because your mind sees your efforts, and it will open up other dimensions to solve.

It is like imagining the route to a destination is not better than reaching it. You complete that task, and your mind will be ready to solve that problem unless your mind is unnecessarily involved in some things and thoughts far from reality. So, it is better to be practical in some situations.

"Problems came to realize our inner potential. Consider it as an opportunity to grow."

Making Some Space

Let us consider a cup entirely filled with water. If I want to pour some other things(like juice), it will overflow. It will not accept the juice because it is filled with water. Similarly, our brain stores some memories firmly based on our past experiences. Our mind subconsciously accepts these experiences. Based on these experiences, we will only make some important decisions.

But the question is, how updated are these experiences? If it works for you, then can it work for everyone? How can you compete for your experience with the whole world? Is it worth working with these experiences?

Such questions we often have to ask ourselves. These questions only keep us updated in this current world. These make us think about our loopholes and open our minds to new things. You may master solving some problems, but if it becomes outdated, what is the use of the mastery achieved in that?

Accepting this and moving on is the best option here. It will make our minds open to new things. These new things will keep us fresh. Again, while learning these new things, we may make mistakes. It is natural to make mistakes in this phase for better learning. Don't hesitate to make mistakes here. In the learning phase, everything will not go smoothly. We have to be ready for some ups and downs. Change is life. If we are stagnant water, chances are it will spoil, but when we become like flowing water, We remain fresh and circulating for all the life on the planet. It will all happen by emptying space for new things. Accepting new knowledge is a crucial way to achieve success.

“Accept the change because change is life.”

Overcoming the Comparison Trauma

Comparison kills the motivation to do work. It applies to those people who spend more time in comparison than to execute that work. It creates stress in your mind, and that leads to unhappy life.

The school or our education system itself nurtures this mentality. For example, of 50 students, 5 will be brilliant in their studies, 35 will be average, and 10 will be below average. However, the school system always highlights brilliant students and sets its standards for all the other students. It is good to give examples of brilliant students; I am not against them. It is one way to make students realize their potential and move towards progress. The problem is how a student's mindset will work here.

Just think for a few minutes about the below-average students. They now fix their mind to become brilliant students. Intelligence towards any subject depends on many factors: their upbringing in their home, parent's support, heredity, extra tuition classes, and kid's interest in learning. It is not possible to quickly become something, but at that young age, those kids will not understand this point. Those kids sincerely try to excel in their studies for one or two months. They will believe this is not their work if they don't find any results. They strongly believe they can't learn anything and are not made for this. This thought will grow as time passes and become their belief system one day. It may convert to trauma as well. The key is that we don't have the skills to learn things. For some, it takes three months; for others, it takes one year. If we had given as much time without thinking about the initial results, we would have realized to crack that work one or the other day. But comparing with high standards will empty our motivation to work.

Let us see nature and how unique it created us. All have different fingerprints, thoughts, and visions of life. Perfection is not about beating all the competition to become the best. It is repairing yourself from the inside and learning to make you the best in the world. Don't compare your work with anyone. Have a brief idea about the world and learn about the competition level, but don't allow the world to interfere with your work. Try to bring the uniqueness outside you. If you have a unique approach, your efforts will create a difference with your competitors. Don't be bound yourself to small things. Only the universe should be your limitation. So your intelligence also helps you achieve this fast. It is about how quickly you deliver unimaginable things to the world with your uniqueness. That is the basic block for anyone to achieve something in this world.

"Comparison is the biggest disease in humanity. Avoid it before occupying you. Uniqueness is the only medicine on your side."

Serving As Many As Possible

How do we do our work without comparison and distractions?

Everybody has a different approach to work. I appreciate everyone's efforts. Whatever work we do, the main thing is how we help/serve people to overcome their problems. Who solves better? That person rules that industry. That is where your approach matters. Here, we are in an ecosystem. For example, if I give better water and needful nourishment to plants in my garden, they will provide me with fresh air, a healthy atmosphere, and better food. It is one example, but this ecosystem relates to every action you take. Your actions will definitely hit your surrounding environment. But, the question is how they are. Are they improving your surroundings? Are they troubling your surroundings?

Don't forget that you impact your surroundings, and your surroundings will definitely affect you. Whatever you give, you will receive. Do your work with ultimate devotion like you are doing prayer to God. Give your work a purest soul, heart, and body. This righteousness is required while we are doing any work. This righteousness will make you love your surroundings. As you love your surroundings, then you will absolutely care about it. So you will get love and care from your surroundings. These surroundings can be anything, such as people, places, states, countries, or the world. There is no limit to this.

Most successful people will have this mindset. They serve people, and they serve as many as they can. We have leaders who are loved by the whole nation. We have scientists who are admired by the entire world. We have artists who are praised by all kinds of people. We have actors who don't have boundaries to love people. They give their best to become the best in the world. They serve people, put effort, and give their purest soul, heart, and body to their work. They don't do business here but express their good thoughts. After that, we will do better business, it is another part. But they will only think of doing their best while doing that work. Ultimately, the people's word of mouth will make them famous. So, working with righteousness and serving as many as possible is essential.

"Building a positive ecosystem is in our hands only."

Giving Your 100%

Perfection is being correct about all the decisions you make. We can do 10 projects. How many will win, and how many will fail? It is not in our hands to control our results. It is not possible to be successful at every project we do. Even when we give our 100% effort, it is hard to achieve 100% success. So this may bother many people, and they will feel unnecessary tension. It is better to analyze why it failed and learn from it to prepare for the next level. It is not good to suffer from your failures. That's why the concept of perfection fails. There is no formula for success. There is no secret ingredient, and it will change according to circumstances every time. A world champion also can lose any day. Then, how do we achieve success in every project we do?

There is one way to achieve success in every project we do. That is, “Don’t stick to results, but stick to purpose.” The purpose of finding joy, happiness, and satisfaction in your work. A doctor’s work may be hectic for some people, but those who love that work will enjoy it. It is a joy for a doctor to treat his patients anytime. So he has that work satisfaction. So it is essential to love our work; the second thing is don’t attach too much to results. For example, if a scientist dreams day and night about a noble prize, worries about it, and thinks about achieving it. The chances are less that he will get it. But if he works joyfully day and night on his experiments, he may have a high chance of achieving it because he gives all his thinking ability to his one job. All his focus is on his work.

That means I am not telling you to think about results. Yes, we have to think about the end results first. However, you should have an aim and vision for your work, but don't attach to results.

"Think about what happens if you focus all your energy on one thing you love to do."

Let It Happen

Think, how will a workplace be without a boss? How will the condition of that workplace be?

There will be no particular arrangement of thoughts, tasks, goals, and targets. The same happens with our minds as well. The mind has unlimited energy, but it needs to be directed. It requires a strict boss. We have to focus our unlimited energy on a particular work. Let us test our minds. Just think about some problems you faced previously.

How did your mind work at that time?

If you seriously give continuous thoughts to your mind, it deeply analyses it. You may sleep, but your subconscious will not sleep. Day and night, our mind tries to find a solution to every possible situation. Some may get a solution while sleeping, some may get it while working, some may get it while playing, and some may get it on a trip to their favorite place. You may have realized now how powerful our focused thoughts are.

The only thing is, we have to be subconsciously aware of some thoughts, and automatically, it will dig deeper. Our thoughts are like seeds, and our mind is like soil. We must provide fertile soil, and better water is positive to grow its deeper roots. Masters will allow it to go deeper for better knowledge. One day, beautiful flowers will blossom for you and your surroundings.

They fail, they learn, and they grow. So, don't try to be perfect. Perfection will happen if good deeds, good intentions, an intelligent mind, a pure soul, a good heart, and better thoughts are devoted to a single work. Don't worry about executing it.

"Don't try to achieve perfection, let it happen."

Check Out Other Books by Author

- ✓ If you like this book, follow the author for future updates.
- ✓ Please share this with your loved ones.
- ✓ Please give your honest review for this book and encourage the readership.
- ✓ Don't forget to check out other self-help books by the author.

Thank You

www.ingramcontent.com/pod-product-compliance
Lightning Source LLC
LaVergne TN
LVHW040921150826
845672LV00007B/2146
9798896322825